Manual
of
Witchcraft
&
Alchemy

Divvs Iacobvs Diabolicis
Pruestigilis Ante Magvm Sistitvr

Virum Impetravit A Decy
Magus Domnibus Disary adir

Formulas

Incantation Bright oil, pure oil shining oil, the purifying oil of the gods oil which softens the sinews of man.

With the oil of the Incantation of Ea, with the oil of the Incantation of Marduk.

I have made thee drip, with the oil of softening which Ea has given soothing.

Bringeth to a full rolling bubble Then add two drops oil of boil... And a dead man's toe...

Life Potion

Bringeth a full rousing bubble, then add two drops oil of boil and a dead man's toe. Next add a dab of Newt saliva. dash of pox. Stir thrice. One final thing and all is done. Add a piece of thine own tongue Administer one drop to victim and stand back. When victim's life force can be seen inhale the glowing aura.

Spells to Ressurect the Dead

Black Flame Candle Spell:

One all hallows Eve
when the moon is round
A virgin will summon thee
from under the ground.

Golaten omnes saculerem
tuba mirum est

Witches Brew

A covern. In the middle,
a boiling cauldron

Leave I ask of the creator,
Seek an answer that misleads
not. Tell me, signs of the
Creator. Lots of Jumala
instruct me!

         ron go; In the poison'd
         entrails throw. Toad,
         that under cold stone

I beg thee, O Great Adonai,
Eloim, Ariel, Jehovam, exert
Thy beneficence towards me,
and give to this rod as I cut it
the power

Hang us-burn us-what ye
will! Our spirits will
abide here in this hill-One
Hallowed Eve when the moon
is round-A virgin will summon
us from the ground.
I beg thee, O Great Adonai to
place in this wand the power.

Witches Brew

A covern. In the middle,
a boiling cauldron

I Witch: Thrice the brinded cat
hath mew'd.

II Witch: Thrice, and once the
hedgepig whin'd.

III Witch: Harpier cries; 'tis time,
tis time.

I Witch: Round about the cauldron go; In the poison'd
entrails throw. Toad,
that under cold stone

I seek a husband. Sitting here, my hair flowing loose. I am like one positioned before a giant procession, searching for a husband for this woman without a spouse.

O Aryaman! This woman cannot longer bear to attend the marriages of other women.

O Creator, produce for me a suitor, a husband!"

Magicians Pact

To summon demons utterance of the nine divine and mystic names:

Eheieh - Jod
El - Shaddai
Tetragrammaton
Elohim Gibor
Eloah VaDaath
Elohim Tzabaoth
Adonai Tzabaoth

Miracles
of
Witchcraft

Miracles occured by simple faith and plateaus devotion, not by incantations and spells composed by the evil occult art that is called magic or by a name of detestation or superstition. sorcery the honourable term of theurgy.

In Augstine 384- 480AD Ora biblica Ja.

Incantation for Sickness

Ofano, Oblamo, Ospergo.
Hola, Noa Massa.
Light, Beff, Cletemati, Adonai,
Cleona, Florit.
Pax Sax Sarax.
Afa Afca Nostra.
Cerum, Heaium, Lada Fium.

Ojala

Ojal

Oja

Oj

O

Excruciating Punishments

gue
Amnesia
Aching bones

oils
Bunions
Biliousness

arbuncles
Chilblains
Cholera

yspepsia
Diarrhea

Excruciating Punishments

Demons have their own peculiarities, their physical distinctiveness, their functional activities. Some dwell in mines and forests. or on mountain tops Some copulate with humans. Warts...Itching...Crib death.

There are spirits that are created for vengeance and in their fury they lay on cruel torments.

Listen, o blood, instead of flow-
ing instead of pouring
forth thy warm stream.
Newt saliva
Stop, o blood, like a wall,
Stop like a reef in the sea
Dash of pox, stir thrice
Like stiff sedge in the moss,
   like a boulder in the field
One thing more and all is done
   add a bit of thy own tongue.

X

In those that are possess'd
with't there oreflowes
Such mellancholly humour, they
imagine
Themselves to be transformed
into wolves
Steale forth in church-yards in
the dead of night,
And dig dead bodies up; as two
nights since

Listen, o blood, instead of flow-
ing instead of pouring
forth thy warm stream.
Newt saliva
Stop, o blood, like a wall,
Stop like a reef in the sea
Dash of pox, stir thrice
Like stiff sedge in the moss,
  like a boulder in the field
One thing more and all is done
  add a bit of thy own tongue.

Then the aged Vainamoinen, He the great primeval sorcerer, Hastened alder-sticks to cut him, And arranged the sticks in order, And began the lots to shuffle. With his fingers to arrange them. And he spoke the words which follow. And in words like this expressed him:

"Leave I ask of the creator, Seek an answer that misleads not. Tell me, signs of the Creator. Lots of Jumala, instruct me."

Sang a dog with pointed
muzzle
Sang a golden-breasted marten
By his spells a hen created
Thereupon a hawk created.

But the mighty son of Poja
By his spells a wolf
created and upon the floor he
sang him
To devour the fleshy bullock.

Power of Witchcraft
Eternal Life

If I command the moon, it will come down; and if i wish to withhold the day, night will linger over my head; and again, if I wish to embark on the sea, I need no ship; and if I wish to fly through the air, I am freed from my weight.

She undertakes by her incantations to arrest the flow of rivers and turn back the stars in their course.

Formulas

Incantation Bright oil, pure oil shiving oil, the purifying oil of the gods oil which softens the sinews of man.

With the oil of the Incantation of Ea, with the oil of the Incantation of Marduk.

I have made thee drip, with the oil of softening which Ea has given soothing.

Bringeth to a full rolling bubble
Then add two drops oil of boil...
And a dead man's toe...

Life Potion

Bringeth a full rousing bubble, then add two drops oil of boil and a dead man's toe. Next add a dab of Newt saliva. dash of pox. Stir thrice. One final thing and all is done. Add a piece of thine own tongue Administer one drop to victim and stand back. When victim's life force can be seen inhale the glowing aura.

Spells to Ressurect the Dead

Black Flame Candle Spell:

One all hallows Eve
when the moon is round
A virgin will summon thee
from under the ground.

Golaten omnes saculerem
tuba mirum est

Witches Brew

A cavern. In the middle,
a boiling cauldron

Leave I ask of the creator,
Seek an answer that misleads
not. Tell me, signs of the
Creator. Lots of Jumala
instruct me!

        ron go; In the poison'd
        entrails throw. Toad,
        that under cold stone

I beg thee, O Great Adonai,
Eloim, Ariel, Jehovam, exert
Thy beneficence towards me,
and give to this rod as I cut it
the power

Hang us-burn us-what ye
will! Our spirits will
abide here in this hill-One
Hallowed Eve when the moon
is round-A virgin will summon
us from the ground.
I beg thee, O Great Adonai to
place in this wand the power.

Witches Brew

A covern. In the middle,
a boiling cauldron

I Witch: Thrice the brinded cat
hath mew'd.

II Witch: Thrice, and once the
hedgepig whin'd.

III Witch: Harpier cries; 'tis time,
tis time.

I Witch: Round about the cauldron go; In the poison'd
entrails throw. Toad,
that under cold stone

I seek a husband. Sitting here, my hair flowing loose. I am like one positioned before a giant procession, searching for a husband for this woman with out a spouse.

O Aryaman! This woman cannot longer bear to attend the marriages of other women.

O Creator, produce for me a suitor, a husband!"

Magicians Pact

To summon demons utter-
ance of the nine divine and
mystic names:

Eheieh – Jod
El – Shaddai
Tetragrammaton
Elohim Gibor
Eloah VaDaath
Elohim Tzabaoth
Adonai Tzabaoth

Miracles
of
Witchcraft

Miracles occured by simple faith and plateaus devotion, not by incantations and spells composed by the evil occult art that is called magic or by a name of detestation or superstition. sorcery the honourable term of theurgy.

In Augstine 384- 480AD

Ora biblica Ja.

Incantation for Sickness

Ofano, Oblamo, Ospergo.
Hola, Noa Massa.
Light, Beff, Cletemati, Adonai,
Cleona, Florit.
Pax Sax Sarax.
Afa Afca Nostra.
Cerum, Heaium, Lada Fium.

      Ojala

      Ojal

      Oja

      Oj

      O

Excruciating Punishments

 gue
Amnesia
Aching bones

 oils
Bunions
Biliousness

 arbuncles
Chilblains
Cholera

 yspepsia
Diarrhea

Excruciating Punishments

Demons have their own peculiarities, their physical distinctiveness, their functional activities. Some dwell in mines and forests. or on mountain tops Some copulate with humans. Warts...Itching...Crib death. There are spirits that are created for vengeance and in their fury they lay on cruel torments.

Listen, o blood, instead of flow‑
ing instead of pouring
forth thy warm stream.
Newt saliva
Stop, o blood, like a wall,
Stop like a reef in the sea
Dash of pox, stir thrice
Like stiff sedge in the moss,
   like a boulder in the field
One thing more and all is done
   add a bit of thy own tongue.

X

In those that are possess'd
with't there oreflowes
Such mellancholly humour, they
imagine
Themselves to be transformed
into wolves
Steale forth in church-yards in
the dead of night,
And dig dead bodies up: as two
nights since

Listen, o blood, instead of flow-
ing instead of pouring
forth thy warm stream.
Newt saliva
Stop, o blood, like a wall,
Stop like a reef in the sea
Dash of pox, stir thrice
Like stiff sedge in the moss,
like a boulder in the field
One thing more and all is done
add a bit of thy own tongue.

Then the aged Vainamoinen, He the great primeval sorcerer, Hastened alder-sticks to cut him, And arranged the sticks in order, And began the lots to shuffle. With his fingers to arrange them. And he spoke the words which follow. And in words like this expressed him:

"Leave I ask of the creator, Seek an answer that misleads not. Tell me, signs of the Creator. Lots of Jumala, instruct me."

Sang a dog with pointed
muzzle
Sang a golden-breasted marten
By his spells a hen created
Thereupon a hawk created.

But the mighty son of Poja
By his spells a wolf
created and upon the floor he
sang him
To devour the fleshy bullock.

Power of Witchcraft
Eternal Life

If I command the moon, it will come down; and if i wish to withhold the day, night will linger over my head; and again, if I wish to embark on the sea, I need no ship; and if I wish to fly through the air, I am freed from my weight.

She undertakes by her incantations to arrest the flow of rivers and turn back the stars in their course.

Formulas

Incantation Bright oil, pure oil shining oil, the purifying oil of the gods oil which softens the sinews of man.

With the oil of the Incantation of Ea, with the oil of the Incantation of Marduk.

I have made thee drip, with the oil of softening which Ea has given soothing.

Bringeth to a full rolling bubble Then add two drops oil of boil... And a dead man's toe...

Life Potion

Bringeth a full rousing bubble, then add two drops oil of boil and a dead man's toe. Next add a dab of Newt saliva. dash of pox. Stir thrice. One final thing and all is done. Add a piece of thine own tongue Administer one drop to victim and stand back. When victim's life force can be seen inhale the glowing aura.

Spells to Ressurect the Dead

Black Flame Candle Spell:

One all hallows Eve
when the moon is round
A virgin will summon thee
from under the ground.

Golaten omnes saculerem
tuba mirum est

Witches Brew

A covern. In the middle,
a boiling cauldron

Leave I ask of the creator,
Seek an answer that misleads
not. Tell me, signs of the
Creator. Lots of Jumala
instruct me!

ron go; In the poison'd
entrails throw. Toad,
that under cold stone

I beg thee, O Great Adonai,
Eloim, Ariel, Jehovam, exert
Thy beneficence towards me,
and give to this rod as I cut it
the power

Hang us-burn us-what ye
will! Our spirits will
abide here in this hill-One
Hallowed Eve when the moon
is round-A virgin will summon
us from the ground.
I beg thee, O Great Adonai to
place in this wand the power.

Witches Brew

A covern. In the middle, a boiling cauldron

I Witch: Thrice the brinded cat
hath mew'd.

II Witch: Thrice, and once the
hedgepig whin'd.

III Witch: Harpier cries; 'tis time,
tis time.

I Witch: Round about the cauldron go; In the poison'd
entrails throw. Toad,
that under cold stone

I seek a husband. Sitting here, my hair flowing loose. I am like one positioned before a giant procession, searching for a husband for this woman with out a spouse.

O Aryaman! This woman cannot longer bear to attend the marriages of other women.

O Creator, produce for me a suitor, a husband!"

Magicians Pact

To summon demons utter-ance of the nine divine and mystic names:

Eheieh ~ Jod
El ~ Shaddai
Tetragrammaton
Elohim Gibor
Eloah Va Daath
Elohim Tzabaoth
Adonai Tzabaoth

Miracles
of
Witchcraft

Miracles occured by simple faith and plateaus devotion, not by incantations and spells composed by the evil occult art that is called magic or by a name of detestation or superstition. sorcery the honourable term of theurgy.

In Augstine 384- 480AD Ora biblica Ja.

Incantation for Sickness

Ofano, Oblamo, Ospergo.
Hola, Noa Massa.
Light, Beff, Cletemati, Adonai,
Cleona, Florit.
Pax Sax Sarax.
Afa Afca Nostra.
Cerum, Heaium, Lada Fium.

      Ojala

      Ojal

      Oja

      Oj

      O

Excruciating Punishments

gue
Amnesia
Aching bones

oils
Bunions
Biliousness

arbuncles
Chilblains
Cholera

yspepsia
Diarrhea

Excruciating Punishments

Demons have their own peculiarities, their physical distinctiveness, their functional activities. Some dwell in mines and forests. or on mountain tops Some copulate with humans. Warts...Itching...Crib death. There are spirits that are created for vengeance and in their fury they lay on cruel torments.

Listen, o blood, instead of flow-
ing instead of pouring
forth thy warm stream.
Newt saliva
Stop, o blood, like a wall,
Stop like a reef in the sea
Dash of pox, stir thrice
Like stiff sedge in the moss,
   like a boulder in the field
One thing more and all is done
   add a bit of thy own tongue.

X

In those that are possess'd
with't there oreflowes
Such mellancholly humour, they
imagine
Themselves to be transformed
into wolves
Steale forth in church-yards in
the dead of night,
And dig dead bodies up: as two
nights since

Listen, o blood, instead of flow-
ing instead of pouring
forth thy warm stream.
Newt saliva
Stop, o blood, like a wall,
Stop like a reef in the sea
Dash of pox, stir thrice
Like stiff sedge in the moss,
  like a boulder in the field
One thing more and all is done
  add a bit of thy own tongue.

Then the aged Vainamoinen, He the great primeval sorcerer, Hastened alder-sticks to cut him, And arranged the sticks in order, And began the lots to shuffle. With his fingers to arrange them. And he spoke the words which follow. And in words like this expressed him:

"Leave I ask of the creator, Seek an answer that misleads not. Tell me, signs of the Creator. Lots of Jumala, instruct me."

Sang a dog with pointed
muzzle
Sang a golden-breasted marten
By his spells a hen created
Thereupon a hawk created.

But the mighty son of Poja
By his spells a wolf
created and upon the floor he
sang him
To devour the fleshy bullock.

Power of Witchcraft
Eternal Life

If I command the moon, it will come down; and if i wish to withhold the day, night will linger over my head; and again, if I wish to embark on the sea, I need no ship; and if I wish to fly through the air, I am freed from my weight.

She undertakes by her incantations to arrest the flow of rivers and turn back the stars in their course.

Formulas

Incantation Bright oil, pure oil shining oil, the purifying oil of the gods oil which softens the sinews of man.

With the oil of the Incantation of Ea, with the oil of the Incantation of Marduk.

I have made thee drip, with the oil of softening which Ea has given soothing.

Bringeth to a full rolling bubble Then add two drops oil of boil... And a dead man's toe...

Life Potion

Bringeth a full rousing bubble, then add two drops oil of boil and a dead man's toe. Next add a dab of Newt saliva. dash of pox. Stir thrice. One final thing and all is done. Add a piece of thine own tongue Administer one drop to victim and stand back. When victim's life force can be seen inhale the glowing aura.

Spells to Ressurect the Dead

Black Flame Candle Spell:

One all hallows Eve
when the moon is round
A virgin will summon thee
from under the ground.

Golaten omnes saculerem
tuba mirum est

Witches Brew

A cavern. In the middle,
a boiling cauldron

Leave I ask of the creator,
Seek an answer that misleads
not. Tell me, signs of the
Creator. Lots of Jumala
instruct me!

ron go; In the poison'd
entrails throw. Toad,
that under cold stone

I beg thee, O Great Adonai,
Eloim, Ariel, Jehovam, exert
Thy beneficence towards me,
and give to this rod as I cut it
the power

Hang us-burn us-what ye
will! Our spirits will
abide here in this hill-One
Hallowed Eve when the moon
is round-A virgin will summon
us from the ground.
I beg thee, O Great Adonai to
place in this wand the power.

Witches Brew

A covern. In the middle, a boiling cauldron

I Witch: Thrice the brinded cat hath mew'd.

II Witch: Thrice, and once the hedgepig whin'd.

III Witch: Harpier cries; 'tis time, tis time.

I Witch: Round about the cauldron go; In the poison'd entrails throw. Toad, that under cold stone

I seek a husband. Sitting here, my hair flowing loose. I am like one positioned before a giant procession, searching for a husband for this woman with out a spouse.

O Aryaman! This woman cannot longer bear to attend the marriages of other women.

O Creator, produce for me a suitor, a husband!"

Magicians Pact

To summon demons utter-ance of the nine divine and mystic names:

Eheieh - Jod
El - Shaddai
Tetragrammaton
Elohim Gibor
Eloah VaDaath
Elohim Tzabaoth
Adonai Tzabaoth

Miracles
of
Witchcraft

Miracles occured by simple faith and plateaus devotion, not by incantations and spells composed by the evil occult art that is called magic or by a name of detestation or superstition. sorcery the honourable term of theurgy.

In Augstine 384- 480AD
Ora biblica Ja.

Incantation for Sickness

Ofano, Oblamo, Ospergo.
Hola, Noa Massa.
Light, Beff, Cletemati, Adonai,
Cleona, Florit.
Pax Sax Sarax.
Afa Afca Nostra.
Cerum, Heaium, Lada Fium.

Ojala

Ojal

Oja

Oj

O

Excruciating Punishments

gue
Amnesia
Aching bones

oils
Bunions
Biliousness

arbuncles
Chilblains
Cholera

yspepsia
Diarrhea

Excruciating Punishments

Demons have their own peculiarities, their physical distinctiveness, their functional activities. Some dwell in mines and forests. or on mountain tops Some copulate with humans. Warts...Itching...Crib death.

There are spirits that are created for vengeance and in their fury they lay on cruel torments.

Listen, o blood, instead of flow-
ing instead of pouring
forth thy warm stream.
Newt saliva
Stop, o blood, like a wall,
Stop like a reef in the sea
Dash of pox, stir thrice
Like stiff sedge in the moss,
   like a boulder in the field
One thing more and all is done
   add a bit of thy own tongue.

X

n those that are possess'd
with't there oreflowes
Such mellancholly humour, they
imagine
Themselves to be transformed
into wolves
Steale forth in church-yards in
the dead of night,
And dig dead bodies up: as two
nights since

Listen, o blood, instead of flow-
ing instead of pouring
forth thy warm stream.
Newt saliva
Stop, o blood, like a wall,
Stop like a reef in the sea
Dash of pox, stir thrice
Like stiff sedge in the moss,
  like a boulder in the field
One thing more and all is done
  add a bit of thy own tongue.

Then the aged Vainamoinen, He the great primeval sorcerer, Hastened alder-sticks to cut him, And arranged the sticks in order, And began the lots to shuffle. With his fingers to arrange them. And he spoke the words which follow. And in words like this expressed him:

"Leave I ask of the creator, Seek an answer that misleads not. Tell me, signs of the Creator. Lots of Jumala, instruct me."

Sang a dog with pointed
muzzle
Sang a golden-breasted marten
By his spells a hen created
Thereupon a hawk created.

But the mighty son of Poja
By his spells a wolf
created and upon the floor he
sang him
To devour the fleshy bullock.

Power of Witchcraft
Eternal Life

If I command the moon, it will come down; and if i wish to withhold the day, night will linger over my head; and again, if I wish to embark on the sea, I need no ship; and if I wish to fly through the air, I am freed from my weight.

She undertakes by her incantations to arrest the flow of rivers and turn back the stars in their course.

Formulas

Incantation Bright oil, pure oil shiving oil, the purifying oil of the gods oil which softens the sinews of man.

With the oil of the Incantation of Ea, with the oil of the Incantation of Marduk.

I have made thee drip, with the oil of softening which Ea has given soothing.

Bringeth to a full rolling bubble
Then add two drops oil of boil...
And a dead man's toe...

Life Potion

Bringeth a full rousing bubble, then add two drops oil of boil and a dead man's toe. Next add a dab of Newt saliva. dash of pox. Stir thrice. One final thing and all is done. Add a piece of thine own tongue Administer one drop to victim and stand back. When victim's life force can be seen inhale the glowing aura.

Spells to Ressurect the Dead

Black Flame Candle Spell:

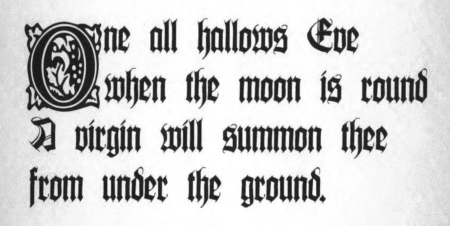

One all hallows Eve
when the moon is round
A virgin will summon thee
from under the ground.

Golaten omnes saculerem
tuba mirum est

Witches Brew

A covern. In the middle, a boiling cauldron

Leave I ask of the creator,
Seek an answer that misleads
not. Tell me, signs of the
Creator. Lots of Jumala
instruct me!

ron go; In the poison'd
entrails throw. Toad,
that under cold stone

I beg thee, O Great Adonai,
Eloim, Ariel, Jehovam, exert
Thy beneficence towards me,
and give to this rod as I cut it
the power

Hang us-burn us-what ye
will! Our spirits will
abide here in this hill-One
Hallowed Eve when the moon
is round-A virgin will summon
us from the ground.
I beg thee, O Great Adonai to
place in this wand the power.

Witches Brew

A covern. In the middle,
a boiling cauldron

I Witch: Thrice the brinded cat
hath mew'd.

II Witch: Thrice, and once the
hedgepig whin'd.

III Witch: Harpier cries; 'tis time,
tis time.

I Witch: Round about the cauldron go; In the poison'd
entrails throw. Toad,
that under cold stone

I seek a husband. Sitting here, my hair flowing loose. I am like one positioned before a giant procession, searching for a husband for this woman without a spouse.

O Aryaman! This woman cannot longer bear to attend the marriages of other women.

O Creator, produce for me a suitor, a husband!"

Magicians Pact

To summon demons utter-ance of the nine divine and mystic names:

Eheieh - Jod
El - Shaddai
Tetragrammaton
Elohim Gibor
Eloah Va Daath
Elohim Tzabaoth
Adonai Tzabaoth

Miracles
of
Witchcraft

Miracles occured by simple faith and plateaus devotion, not by incantations and spells composed by the evil occult art that is called magic or by a name of detestation or superstition. sorcery the honourable term of theurgy.

In Augstine 384- 480AD
Ora biblica Ja.

Incantation for Sickness

Ofano, Oblamo, Ospergo.
Hola, Noa Massa.
Light, Beff, Cletemati, Adonai,
Cleona, florit.
Pax Sax Sarax.
Afa Afca Nostra.
Cerum, Heaium, Lada fium.

Ojala

Ojal

Oja

Oj

O

Excruciating Punishments

gue
Amnesia
Aching bones

oils
Bunions
Biliousness

arbuncles
Chilblains
Cholera

yspepsia
Diarrhea

Excruciating Punishments

Demons have their own peculiarities, their physical distinctiveness, their functional activities. Some dwell in mines and forests. or on mountain tops Some copulate with humans. Warts...Itching...Crib death. There are spirits that are created for vengeance and in their fury they lay on cruel torments.

Listen, o blood, instead of flow-
ing instead of pouring
forth thy warm stream.
Newt saliva
Stop, o blood, like a wall,
Stop like a reef in the sea
Dash of pox, stir thrice
Like stiff sedge in the moss,
  like a boulder in the field
One thing more and all is done
  add a bit of thy own tongue.

X

In those that are possess'd
with't there oreflowes
Such mellancholly humour, they
imagine
Themselves to be transformed
into wolves
Steale forth in church-yards in
the dead of night,
And dig dead bodies up: as two
nights since

Listen, o blood, instead of flow-
ing instead of pouring
forth thy warm stream.
Newt saliva
Stop, o blood, like a wall,
Stop like a reef in the sea
Dash of pox, stir thrice
Like stiff sedge in the moss,
like a boulder in the field
One thing more and all is done
add a bit of thy own tongue.

Then the aged Vainamoinen, He the great primeval sorcerer, Hastened alder-sticks to cut him, And arranged the sticks in order, And began the lots to shuffle. With his fingers to arrange them. And he spoke the words which follow. And in words like this expressed him:

"Leave I ask of the creator, Seek an answer that misleads not. Tell me, signs of the Creator. Lots of Jumala, instruct me."

Sang a dog with pointed muzzle
Sang a golden-breasted marten
By his spells a hen created
Thereupon a hawk created.

But the mighty son of Poja
By his spells a wolf
created and upon the floor he
sang him
To devour the fleshy bullock.

Power of Witchcraft
Eternal Life

If I command the moon, it will come down; and if i wish to withhold the day, night will linger over my head; and again, if I wish to embark on the sea, I need no ship; and if I wish to fly through the air, I am freed from my weight.

She undertakes by her incantations to arrest the flow of rivers and turn back the stars in their course.

Formulas

Incantation Bright oil, pure oil shiving oil, the purifying oil of the gods oil which softens the sinews of man.

With the oil of the Incantation of Ea, with the oil of the Incantation of Marduk.

I have made thee drip, with the oil of softening which Ea has given soothing.

Bringeth to a full rolling bubble Then add two drops oil of boil...

And a dead man's toe...

Life Potion

Bringeth a full rousing bubble, then add two drops oil of boil and a dead man's toe. Next add a dab of Newt saliva. dash of pox. Stir thrice. One final thing and all is done. Add a piece of thine own tongue Administer one drop to victim and stand back. When victim's life force can be seen inhale the glowing aura.

Spells to Ressurect the Dead

Black Flame Candle Spell:

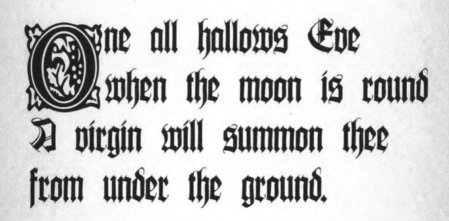

One all hallows Eve
when the moon is round
A virgin will summon thee
from under the ground.

Golaten omnes saculerem
tuba mirum est

Witches Brew

A cavern. In the middle,
a boiling cauldron

Leave I ask of the creator,
Seek an answer that misleads
not. Tell me, signs of the
Creator. Lots of Jumala
instruct me!

ron go; In the poison'd
entrails throw. Toad,
that under cold stone

I beg thee, O Great Adonai,
Eloim, Ariel, Jehovam, exert
Thy beneficence towards me,
and give to this rod as I cut it
the power

Hang us–burn us–what ye
will! Our spirits will
abide here in this hill–One
Hallowed Eve when the moon
is round–A virgin will summon
us from the ground.
I beg thee, O Great Adonai to
place in this wand the power.

Witches Brew

A covern. In the middle,
a boiling cauldron

I Witch: Thrice the brinded cat
hath mew'd.

II Witch: Thrice, and once the
hedgepig whin'd.

III Witch: Harpier cries; 'tis time,
tis time.

I Witch: Round about the cauldron go; In the poison'd
entrails throw. Toad,
that under cold stone

I seek a husband. Sitting here, my hair flowing loose. I am like one positioned before a giant procession, searching for a husband for this woman without a spouse.

O Aryaman! This woman cannot longer bear to attend the marriages of other women.

O Creator, produce for me a suitor, a husband!"

Magicians Pact

To summon demons utterance of the nine divine and mystic names:

Eheieh - Jod
El - Shaddai
Tetragrammaton
Elohim Gibor
Eloah VaDaath
Elohim Tzabaoth
Adonai Tzabaoth

Miracles of Witchcraft

Miracles occured by simple faith and plateaus devotion, not by incantations and spells composed by the evil occult art that is called magic or by a name of detestation or superstition. sorcery the honourable term of theurgy.

In Augstine 384- 480AD
Ora biblica Ja.

Incantation for Sickness

Ofano, Oblamo, Ospergo.
Hola, Noa Massa.
Light, Beff, Cletemati, Adonai,
Cleona, Florit.
Pax Sax Sarax.
Afa Afca Nostra.
Cerum, Heaium, Lada Fium.
Ojala
Ojal
Oja
Oj
O

Excruciating Punishments

gue
Amnesia
Aching bones

oils
Bunions
Biliousness

arbuncles
Chilblains
Cholera

yspepsia
Diarrhea

Excruciating Punishments

Demons have their own peculiarities, their physical distinctiveness, their functional activities. Some dwell in mines and forests. or on mountain tops Some copulate with humans. Warts...Itching...Crib death. There are spirits that are created for vengeance and in their fury they lay on cruel torments.

Listen, o blood, instead of flow-
ing instead of pouring
forth thy warm stream.
Newt saliva
Stop, o blood, like a wall,
Stop like a reef in the sea
Dash of pox, stir thrice
Like stiff sedge in the moss,
 like a boulder in the field
One thing more and all is done
 add a bit of thy own tongue.

X

n those that are possess'd
with't there oreflowes
Such mellancholly humour, they
imagine
Themselves to be transformed
into wolves
Steale forth in church-yards in
the dead of night,
And dig dead bodies up: as two
nights since

Listen, o blood, instead of flow-
ing instead of pouring
forth thy warm stream.
Newt saliva
Stop, o blood, like a wall,
Stop like a reef in the sea
Dash of pox, stir thrice
Like stiff sedge in the moss,
    like a boulder in the field
One thing more and all is done
    add a bit of thy own tongue.

Then the aged Vainamoinen, He the great primeval sorcerer, Hastened alder-sticks to cut him, And arranged the sticks in order, And began the lots to shuffle. With his fingers to arrange them. And he spoke the words which follow. And in words like this expressed him:

"Leave I ask of the creator, Seek an answer that misleads not. Tell me, signs of the Creator. Lots of Jumala, instruct me."

Sang a dog with pointed muzzle
Sang a golden-breasted marten
By his spells a hen created
Thereupon a hawk created.

But the mighty son of Poja
By his spells a wolf
created and upon the floor he
sang him
To devour the fleshy bullock.

Power of Witchcraft
Eternal Life

If I command the moon, it will come down; and if i wish to withhold the day, night will linger over my head; and again, if I wish to embark on the sea, I need no ship; and if I wish to fly through the air, I am freed from my weight.

She undertakes by her incantations to arrest the flow of rivers and turn back the stars in their course.

Formulas

Incantation Bright oil, pure oil shining oil, the purifying oil of the gods oil which softens the sinews of man.

With the oil of the Incantation of Ea, with the oil of the Incantation of Marduk.

I have made thee drip, with the oil of softening which Ea has given soothing.

Bringeth to a full rolling bubble Then add two drops oil of boil... And a dead man's toe...

Life Potion

Bringeth a full rousing bubble, then add two drops oil of boil and a dead man's toe. Next add a dab of Newt saliva. dash of pox. Stir thrice. One final thing and all is done. Add a piece of thine own tongue Administer one drop to victim and stand back. When victim's life force can be seen inhale the glowing aura.

Spells to Ressurect the Dead

Black Flame Candle Spell:

One all hallows Eve
when the moon is round
A virgin will summon thee
from under the ground.

Golaten omnes saculerem
tuba mirum est

Witches Brew

A covern. In the middle, a boiling cauldron

Leave I ask of the creator, Seek an answer that misleads not. Tell me, signs of the Creator. Lots of Jumala instruct me!

ron go; In the poison'd entrails throw. Toad, that under cold stone

I beg thee, O Great Adonai,
Eloim, Ariel, Jehovam, exert
Thy beneficence towards me,
and give to this rod as I cut it
the power

Hang us-burn us-what ye
will! Our spirits will
abide here in this hill-One
Hallowed Eve when the moon
is round-A virgin will summon
us from the ground.
I beg thee, O Great Adonai to
place in this wand the power.

Witches Brew

A cavern. In the middle,
a boiling cauldron

I Witch: Thrice the brinded cat
hath mew'd.

II Witch: Thrice, and once the
hedgepig whin'd.

III Witch: Harpier cries; 'tis time,
tis time.

I Witch: Round about the cauldron go; In the poison'd
entrails throw. Toad,
that under cold stone

I seek a husband. Sitting here, my hair flowing loose. I am like one positioned before a giant procession, searching for a husband for this woman without a spouse.

O Aryaman! This woman cannot longer bear to attend the marriages of other women.

O Creator, produce for me a suitor, a husband!"

Magicians Pact

To summon demons utterance of the nine divine and mystic names;

Eheieh – Jod
El – Shaddai
Tetragrammaton
Elohim Gibor
Eloah Va Daath
Elohim Tzabaoth
Adonai Tzabaoth

Miracles
of
Witchcraft

Miracles occured by simple faith and plateaus devotion, not by incantations and spells composed by the evil occult art that is called magic or by a name of detestation or superstition. Sorcery the honourable term of theurgy.

In Augstine 384- 480AD
Ora biblica Ja.

Incantation for Sickness

Ofano, Oblamo, Ospergo.
Hola, Noa Massa.
Light, Beff, Cletemati, Adonai,
Cleona, Florit.
Pax Sax Sarax.
Afa Afca Nostra.
Cerum, Heaium, Lada Fium.
Ojala
Ojal
Oja
Oj
O

Excruciating Punishments

gue
Amnesia
Aching bones

oils
Bunions
Biliousness

arbuncles
Chilblains
Cholera

yspepsia
Diarrhea